PENGUIN BOOKS

Confabulations

John Berger was born in London in 1926. His acclaimed works of fiction and non-fiction include the seminal *Ways of Seeing*; the novel *G.*, which won the Booker Prize in 1972; and, most recently, *Bento's Sketchbook*. He lives in Paris.

JOHN BERGER

Confabulations

PENGUIN BOOKS

PENGUIN BOOKS

UK | USA | Canada | Ireland | Australia
India | New Zealand | South Africa

Penguin Books is part of the Penguin Random House group of companies
whose addresses can be found at global.penguinrandomhouse.com.

Penguin
Random House
UK

First published 2016
002

Copyright © John Berger, 2016

The moral right of the author has been asserted

'Jailhouse Blues'. Words by Clarence Williams. Music by Bessie Smith. © Copyright
1923 Universal MCA Music Publishing (US). All Rights Reserved. International
Copyright Secured. Used by Permission of Music Sales Limited. 'Talking At The
Same Time'. Words & Music by Kathleen Brennan & Thomas Waits © Copyright
2011 Jalma Music (ASCAP). Universal Music Publishing MGB Limited. All Rights
Reserved. International Copyright Secured. Used by Permission of Music Sales
Limited. 'Carrying the Songs' by Moya Cannon (Carrying the Songs, 2007) is
copyrighted and reprinted here by kind permission of Carcanet Press Limited,
Manchester, UK. 'Stone' from Abdulkareem Kasid, Sarabad, translated by the
author and Sara Halub with John Welch (Bristol: Shearsman Books, 2015). Excerpt
from 'Cafés', from Abdulkareem Kasid, Sarabad, translated by the author and
Sara Halub with John Welch (Bristol: Shearsman Books, 2015). Excerpt from 'Cafés',
from Abdulkareem Kasid, Sarabad, translated by the author and Sara Halub with
John Welch (Bristol: Shearsman Books, 2015).

Text Design by Davide Romualdi

Set in 12/16.5 pt Haarlemmer MT Pro
Typeset by Jouve (UK), Milton Keynes
Printed in Italy by Printer Trento Srl

A CIP catalogue record for this book is available from the British Library

ISBN: 978-0-141-98495-7

www.greenpenguin.co.uk

MIX
Paper from
responsible sources
FSC   FSC® C018179
www.fsc.org

Penguin Books is committed to a sustainable
future for our business, our readers and our planet.
This book is made from Forest Stewardship
Council™ certified paper.

CONTENTS

Self-Portrait 1

A Gift for Rosa 9

Impertinence 25

Some Notes about the Art of Falling 31

Et in Arcadia Ego 45

On Vigilance 65

A Meeting Place 73

La Lalala Lalala La 79

Some Notes about Song 91

Pieces of Silver 123

How to Resist a State of Forgetfulness 133

Picture Credits 145

SELF-PORTRAIT

I have been writing for about eighty years. First letters then poems and speeches, later stories and articles and books, now notes.

The activity of writing has been a vital one for me; it helps me to make sense of things and to continue. Writing, however, is an off-shoot of something deeper and more general – our relationship with language as such. And the subject of these few notes is language.

Let's begin by examining the activity of translating from one language to another. Most translations today are technical, whereas I'm referring to literary translations. The translation of texts which concern individual human experience.

The conventional view of translation involves studying the words on one page in one language, then rendering them into another language on another page. This involves a so-called word-for-word translation, then an adaptation to respect and incorporate the linguistic tradition and rules of the second language, and finally another working-over to recreate the equivalent of the 'voice' of the original text. Many, perhaps most, translations follow this procedure and the results are worthy but second-rate.

Why? Because true translation is not a binary affair between two languages but a triangular affair. The third point of the triangle being what lay behind the words of the original text before it was written. True translation demands a return to the pre-verbal.

We read and reread the words of the original text in order to penetrate through them, to reach, to touch the vision or experience which prompted them. We then gather up what we have found there and take this quivering almost wordless 'thing' and place it behind the language into which it needs to be translated. And now the principal task is to persuade the host language to take in and welcome the 'thing' which is waiting to be articulated.

This practice reminds us that a language cannot be reduced to a dictionary or stock of words and phrases. Nor can it be reduced to a warehouse of the works written in it.

A spoken language is a body, a living creature, whose physiognomy is verbal and whose visceral functions are linguistic. And this creature's home is the inarticulate as well as the articulate.

Consider the term Mother Tongue. In Russian the term is *Rodnoi-yazyk*, which means Nearest or Dearest Tongue. At a pinch one could call it Darling Tongue.

Mother Tongue is our first language, first heard as infants from the mouths of our mothers. Hence the logic of the term.

I mention it now because the creature of language, which I'm trying to describe, is undoubtedly feminine. I imagine its centre as a phonetic uterus.

Within one Mother Tongue are all Mother Tongues. Or, to put it another way: every Mother Tongue is universal.

Noam Chomsky has brilliantly demonstrated

that all languages – not only verbal ones – have certain structures and procedures in common. And so a Mother Tongue is related to (rhymes with?) non-verbal languages – such as the languages of signs, of behaviour, of spatial accommodation.

When I'm drawing, I try to unravel and transcribe a *text* of appearances, which already has, I know, its indescribable but assured place in my Mother Tongue.

Words, terms, phrases can be separated from the creature of their language and used as mere labels. They then become inert and empty.

Texte Olivier

The repetitive use of acronyms is a simple example of this. Most mainstream political discourse today is composed of words which, separated from any creature of language, are inert and dead. And such dead 'word-mongering' wipes out memory and breeds a ruthless complacency.

What has prompted me to write over the years is the hunch that something needs to be told and that, if I don't try to tell it, it risks not being told. I picture myself not so much a consequential, professional writer, as a stop-gap man.

After I've written a few lines I let the words slip back into the creature of their language. And there, they are instantly recognized and greeted by a host of other words, with whom they have an affinity of meaning, or of opposition, or of metaphor or alliteration or rhythm. I listen to their confabulation. Together they are contesting the use to which I put the words I chose. They are questioning the roles I allotted them.

So I modify the lines, change a word or two, and submit them again. Another confabulation begins.

And it goes on like this until there is a low murmur of provisional consent. Then I proceed to the next paragraph.

Another confabulation begins . . .

Others can place me as they like as a writer. For myself I'm the son of a bitch – and you can guess who the bitch is, no?

A GIFT FOR ROSA

Rosa! I've known you since I was a kid. And now I'm twice as old as you were when they battered you to death in January 1919, a few months after you and Karl Liebknecht had founded what would become the German Communist Party.

You often come out of a page I'm reading, and sometimes out of a page I'm trying to write; come out to join me with a toss of your head and a smile. No single page and none of the prison cells they repeatedly put you in could ever contain you.

I want to send you something. Before it was given to me, this object was in the town of Zamosc in south-east Poland. In the town where you were born and where your father was a timber merchant. But the link with you is not as simple as that.

The object belonged to a Polish friend of mine called Janine. She lived alone: not in the elegant main square as you did during the first two years of life, but in a cramped suburban house on the outskirts of the town.

Janine's house and her tiny garden were full of potted plants. There were even potted plants on the floor of her bedroom. And she liked nothing better, when she had a visitor, than to point out, with her elderly working woman's fingers, the special particularity of each one of her plants. Her plants kept her company. She gossiped and joked with them.

Although I don't speak Polish, the European country I perhaps feel most at home in is Poland. I share with Poles something like their order of priorities. Most of them are not intrigued by power because they have lived through every conceivable kind of power-shit. They are experts about finding a way round obstacles. They continually invent ploys for getting by. They respect secrets. They have long memories. They make sorrel soup from wild sorrel. They want to be cheerful.

You say something similar in one of your angry letters from prison. Self-pity always made you angry and you were replying to a moaning letter from a friend. 'To be a human being', you say, 'is the main thing above all else. And that means to be firm and clear and cheerful, yes, cheerful in spite of everything and anything, because howling is the business of the weak. To be a human being means to joyfully toss your entire life in the giant scales of fate if it must be so, and at the same time to rejoice in the brightness of every day and the beauty of every cloud.'

In Poland during recent years a new trade has developed and anyone who practises it is called a Stacz, which means 'taking the place'. One pays a man or a woman to join a queue and after a very long while (most queues are very long) when the Stacz is near to the head of the queue one takes his or her place. The queues may be for food, a kitchen utensil, some kind of licence, a government stamp on a document, sugar, rubber boots . . .

They invent many ploys for getting by.

In the early 1970s, my friend Janine decided to take a train to Moscow, as several of her neighbours had recently done. It was not an easy decision to take. Only a year or two before, in 1970, there had been the massacre at Gdansk and other seaports, where hundreds of shipbuilding workers on strike had been shot down by Polish soldiers and police under orders from Moscow.

You foresaw it, Rosa, the dangers implicit in the Bolshevik manner of arguing all reasoning; you already foresaw it in 1918, in your commentary on the Russian Revolution. 'Freedom only for the members of the government, only for the members of the Party – though they are quite numerous – is no freedom at all. Freedom is always the freedom of the one who thinks differently. Not because of any fanatical concept of justice, but because all that is instructive, wholesome and purifying in political freedom depends on this essential characteristic, and its effectiveness vanishes when "freedom" becomes a special privilege.'

Janine took the train to Moscow to buy gold. Gold cost there a third of what it did in Poland. Leaving the Bielorusski station behind her, she eventually found the backstreet where the licenced jewellers had rings to sell. There was already a long queue of other 'foreign' women waiting to buy. For the sake of law and order each woman had a number chalked on the palm of her hand which indicated her place in the line. A cop was there to chalk the numbers. When Janine eventually reached the counter with her prepared roubles she bought three gold rings.

On her way back to the station she caught sight of the object I want to send to you, Rosa. It cost only 60 Kopek. She bought it on the spur of the moment. It tickled her fancy. It would chat with her potted plants.

She had to wait a long while in the station

for the train back. You knew, Rosa, these Russian stations that become encampments of long-waiting passengers. Janine slipped one of her rings on to the fourth finger of her left hand; the other two she hid in more intimate places. When the train arrived and she climbed up into it, a soldier offered her a corner seat as she sighed with relief: she would be able to sleep. At the frontier she had no problems.

In Zamosc she sold the rings for twice the sum she had paid for them, and they were still considerably cheaper than any which could be bought in a Polish shop. Janine, after deducting her rail fare, had made a little windfall.

The object I want to send you she placed on her kitchen windowsill.

'The goal of an encyclopedia is to assemble all the knowledge scattered on the surface of the earth, to demonstrate the general system to the people with whom we live, and to transmit it to the people who will come after us, so that the works of centuries past is not useless to the centuries which follow, that our descendants by becoming more learned, may become more virtuous and happier . . .'

Diderot is explaining, in 1750, the encyclopedia he has just helped to create.

The object on Janine's windowsill has something encyclopedic about it. It's a thin cardboard box, the size of a quarto sheet of paper. Printed on its lid is a coloured engraving of a Collared Flycatcher, and underneath it two words in Cyrillic Russian: SONG BIRDS.

Open the lid. Inside are three rows of matchboxes, with six boxes to each row. And each box has a label with a coloured engraving of a different song bird. Eighteen different songsters. And below each engraving in very small print the name of the bird in Russian. You who wrote furiously in Russian, Polish and German, would have been able to read them. I can't. I have to guess from my vague memories of sporadic bird-watching.

The satisfaction of identifying a live bird as it flies over, or disappears into a hedgerow, is a strange one, isn't it? It involves a weird, momentary intimacy, as if at that moment of recognition one addresses the bird – despite the din and confusions of countless other events – one addresses it by its very own particular nickname. Wagtail! Wagtail!

Of the eighteen birds on the labels, I perhaps recognize five.

The boxes are full of matches with green striking heads. Sixty in each box: seconds in a minute and minutes in an hour. Each one a potential flame.

'The modern proletarian class', you wrote, 'doesn't carry out its struggle according to a plan set out in some book or theory; the modern worker's struggle is a part of history, a part of social progress, and in the middle of history, in the middle of progress, in the middle of the fight, we learn how we must fight.'

On the lid of the cardboard box there is a short explanatory note addressed to matchbox-label collectors (phillumenists as they are called) in the USSR of the 1970s.

The note gives the following information. In evolutionary terms birds preceded animals, in the world today there are an estimated 5000 species of birds; in the Soviet Union there are 400 species of song birds; in general it is the male birds who sing. Song birds have specially developed vocal chords at the bottom of their throats; they usually nest in bushes, trees or on the ground; they are an aid to cereal agriculture because they eat and thus eliminate hordes of insects. Recently in the remote areas of the Soviet Union three new species of singing sparrows have been identified.

Janine kept the box on her kitchen windowsill. It gave her pleasure and in the winter it reminded her of birds singing.

When you were imprisoned for your vehement opposition to the First World War, you listened to a blue titmouse 'who always stayed close to my window, came with the others to be fed, and diligently sang its funny little song, *tsee-tsee-bay*, but it sounded like the mischievous teasing of a child. It always made me laugh and I would answer with the same call. Then the bird vanished with the others at the beginning of this month, no doubt nesting elsewhere. I had seen and heard nothing of it for weeks. Yesterday its well-known notes came suddenly from the other side of the wall which separates our courtyard from another part of the prison; but it was considerably altered, for the bird called three times in brief succession, *tsee-tsee-bay*, *tsee-tsee-bay*, *tsee-tsee-bay*, and then all was still. It went to my heart, for there was so much conveyed by this hasty call from the distance – a whole history of bird life.'

After several weeks Janine decided to put the box in her cupboard under the stairs. She thought of this cupboard as a kind of shelter, the nearest she had to a cellar, and in it she kept what she called her *reserve*. The reserve consisted of a tin of salt, a tin of cooking sugar, a larger tin of flour, a little sack of Kasha and matches. Most Polish housewives kept such a reserve as a means of minimal survival for the day when suddenly the shops, during some national crisis, would have nothing on their shelves.

The next such crisis would be in 1980. Again it began in Gdansk, where workers went on strike in protest against rising food prices. Their action gave birth to the national movement of Solidarnosc, Solidarity, which brought down the government.

'The modern proletarian class,' you wrote a lifetime earlier, 'doesn't carry out its struggle according to a plan set out in some book or theory: the modern workers' struggle is a part of history, a part of social progress, and in the middle of history, in the middle of progress, in the middle of the fight, we learn how we must fight.'

When Janine died in 2010, her son Witek found the box in the cupboard under the stairs and brought it to Paris, where he was working as a plumber and builder. He brought it to give it to me. We are old friends. Our friendship began by playing cards together evening after evening. We played a Russian and Polish game called *Imbecile*. In this game the first player to *lose* all his or her cards is the winner. Witek guessed that the box would set me wondering.

One of the birds in the second row of matchboxes I recognize as a linnet with his pink breast and his two white streaks on his tail. Tsooeet! Tsooeet! . . . Often several of them sing in chorus from the top of a bush.

'The one who has done the most to restore me to reason is a small friend whose image I am sending enclosed. This comrade with the jauntily held beak, steeply rising forehead, and eye of a know-it-all is called Hypolais hypolais, or in everyday language the arbor bird or also the garden mocker.' You are imprisoned in Poznan in

1917 and you continue your letter like this: 'This bird is quite an oddball. He doesn't sing just one song or one melody like other birds, but he is a public speaker by the grace of God, he holds forth, making his speeches to the garden, and does so with a very loud voice full of dramatic excitement, leaping transitions, and passages of heightened pathos. He brings up the most impossible questions, then hurries to answer them himself, with nonsense, making the most daring assertions, heatedly refuting views that no one has stated, charges through wide open doors, then suddenly exclaims in triumph: "Didn't I say so? Didn't I say so?" Immediately after that he solemnly warns everyone who's willing or not willing to listen: "You'll see! You'll see!" (He has the clever habit of repeating each witty remark twice.)'

The linnet's box, Rosa, is full of matches.

'The masses', you wrote in 1900, 'are in reality their own leader, dialectically creating their own development procedure . . .'

How to send this collection of matchboxes to you? The thugs who killed you, threw your mutilated body into a Berlin canal. It was found in the stagnant water three months later. Some doubted whether it was your corpse.

I can send it to you by writing in this dark time these pages.

'I was, I am, I will be,' you said. You live in your example for us, Rosa. And here it is, I'm sending it to your example.

IMPERTINENCE

I recently reread Albert Camus' wonderful book *The First Man*. In it he searches in his childhood and early years for whatever it was that made him the man and writer he later became. And he does this without a trace of egocentricity. It's a book about the world at that time and about History.

After reading it, I started to ask myself what has made me the kind of storyteller I am. And I came upon a clue. Nothing comparable to what Camus found. Just one insight to note down briefly.

For as long back as I can remember I have had the sensation of being a kind of orphan. A strange kind of orphan, for I had loving parents. There was nothing pathetic about my condition. Certain material circumstances, however, made this sensation possible and even encouraged it.

I seldom saw my parents. When I was at home I was looked after by a New Zealand governess whilst my mother worked in a kitchen making cakes and sweets to sell on the market. This was in the 1930s and my parents had a hard time making ends meet given their way of living. In the two rooms where the Governess and I lived there was a large wardrobe which she called the Cry Cupboard. When I wept I was put in it. From time to time my mother came upstairs to the two rooms to see how we were faring, and to bring us a box of home-made chocolate fudge.

At an early age I was sent to boarding schools. Each term lasted about three months and my parents came to visit me once each term and took me out for a Saturday afternoon.

Our only Family occasion was Christmas. A three-day feast with uncles, aunts, cousins. And from an early age, at the end of the sumptuous Christmas meal, I was asked to address the family assembly and make them laugh, as if I were an oddball messenger from elsewhere.

When I was sixteen I ran away from

boarding school and found a way to live independently with friends in London. And we managed. At Christmas time we'd go down to visit my parents and celebrate. My father gave me my first moped. When I was eighteen I asked him to pose for me and I painted his portrait. When he was a kid he had wanted to be a painter but was not allowed to be. But he kept as a souvenir a painting he had made on a metal plate, a painting of some dahlias, and for me, as a kid, this painted plate was a kind of talisman.

As an orphan one learns to be self-sufficient and one learns the tricks of the trades which go with that. One becomes a free-lance.

As a free-lance, from the age of four or five onwards, I treated all those I encountered as if they too were orphans like me. And I believe I still do this.

I propose a conspiracy of orphans. We exchange winks. We reject hierarchies. All hierarchies. We take the shit of the world for granted and we exchange stories about how we nevertheless get by. We are impertinent. More than half the stars in the universe are orphan-stars belonging to no constellation. And they give off more light than all the constellation stars.

Yes we are impertinent. And I guess that I approach and chat up readers in the same way. As if you too were orphans.

SOME NOTES ABOUT
THE ART OF FALLING

He sees what's happening in the world as something both pitiless and inexplicable. And he takes this for granted. His energy is concentrated on the immediate, on getting by and on finding a way out to something a bit brighter. He has observed that there are many circumstances and situations in life which occur and reoccur and are therefore, despite their strangeness, familiar. Since early childhood he has been familiar with dictums, jokes, hints of advice, tricks of the trade, dodges, which refer to these recurrent daily puzzles of life. And so he faces them with a proverbial foreknowledge of what he's up against. He's seldom nonplussed.

Here are some of the axioms of the proverbial foreknowledge he has acquired.

The arse is the centre of the male body; it's where you first kick your opponent, and it's what you most frequently fall on when knocked down.

Women are another army. Watch above all their eyes.

The powerful are always hefty and nervous.

Preachers love only their own voices.

There are no words to name or explain the daily run of trouble, unmet needs and frustrated desire.

Most people have no time of their own yet they don't realise this. Pursued, they pursue their lives.

You, like them, count for nothing, until you step aside and stick your neck out, then your companions will stop short and gaze in wonder. And in the silence of that wonder there is every conceivable word of every mother tongue. You've created a hiatus of recognition.

The ranks of men and women possessing nothing or almost nothing can offer a spare hole of exactly the right size for a little fellow to hide in.

The digestive system is often beyond our control.

A hat is not a protection from the weather; it's a mark of rank.

When a man's trousers fall down it's a humiliation; when a woman's skirts are uplifted it's an illumination.

In a pitiless world a walking stick may be a companion.

Other axioms apply to location and settings. To enter most buildings money – or evidence of money – is required.

Staircases are slides.

Windows are for throwing things or climbing through.

Balconies are posts from which to scramble down or from which to drop things.

Wild nature is a hiding place.

All chases are circular.

Any step taken is likely to be a mistake, so take it with style to distract from the probable shit.

Something like this was part of the proverbial knowledge of a kid, around ten years old – 10 the first time your age has two numerals – hanging out in south London, in Lambeth, at the very beginning of the twentieth century.

A lot of this childhood was spent in Public Institutions: first a workhouse and then a School for destitute children. Hannah, his mother, to whom he was deeply attached, was incapable of looking after him. During much of her life she was confined to a Lunatic Asylum. She came from a south London milieu of Music-Hall performers.

Public institutions for the destitute, such as Workhouses and School for Derelict Children resembled, still resemble, prisons, in the way they are organized and in the way they are laid out. Penitentiaries for Losers. When I think of that 10-year-old child and what he experienced, I think of the paintings of a certain friend of mine today.

My friend Michel Quanne, until he was in his 40s, spent more than half his life in prison, sentenced for repeated petty larcenies. While in prison he began to paint.

His subjects are stories of happenings in the outside free world, as seen and imagined by a prisoner. A striking feature of these paintings is the anonymity of the places, of the locations

depicted in them. The imagined figures, the pro-
tagonists, are vivid, expressive and energetic, but
the street-corners, the imposing buildings, the
exits and entrances, the sky-lines and alley-ways,
among which the figures find themselves, are
barren, faceless, lifeless, indifferent. Nowhere is
there a hint or trace of any mother-touch.

We are looking at places in the outside world
through the transparent but impenetrable and
pitiless glass of a window in a prison-cell.

The 10-year-old grows into an adolescent,
then a young man. Short, very thin, with piercing

blue eyes. He dances and sings. He also mimes. He mimes inventing elaborate dialogues between the features of his face, the gestures of his fastidious hands and the air surrounding him which is free and belongs nowhere. As a performer he becomes a master pickpocket, hoiking laughter out of pocket after pocket of confusion and despair. He directs films and plays in them. Their sets are barren, anonymous and motherless.

Dear Reader, you've guessed whom I'm referring to, haven't you? Charlie Chaplin, the little Fellow, the Tramp.

While his team were shooting *The Gold Rush* in 1923, there was an agitated discussion going on in the studio about the story-line. And a fly kept distracting their attention, so Chaplin, furious, asked for a swatter and tried to kill it. He failed. After a moment the fly landed on the table beside him, within easy reach. He picked up the swatter to swipe at it, then abruptly stopped and put down the swatter. When the others asked Why?, he looked at them and said: 'It isn't the same fly.'

A decade earlier Roscoe Arbuckle, one of Chaplin's favourite 'hefty' collaborators, remarked that his mate Chaplin was a 'complete comic genius, undoubtedly the only one of our time who will be talked about a century from now.'

The century has passed and what 'Fatty' Arbuckle said has turned out to be true. During that century the world changed deeply – economically, politically, socially. With the invention of 'talkies' and the new edifice of Holly-wood, the cinema also changed. Yet the early Chaplin films have lost none of their surprise or humour or bite or illumination. More than that, their relevance seems closer, more urgent than ever before: They are an intimate commentary on the twenty-first century in which we are living.

How is this possible? I want to offer two insights. The first concerns Chaplin's proverbial view of the world as described above; the second concerns his genius as a clown which paradoxic-ally, owed so much to the tribulations of his childhood.

Today the global tyranny of speculative financial capitalism, which uses national govern-ments as its slave-masters, and the world media as its dope-distributor, this tyranny whose sole aim is profit and ceaseless accumulation, imposes on us a view and pattern of life which is hectic, precarious, merciless, inexplicable. And this view of life is even closer to the 10 year-old's proverbial view of the world than was life at the time the early Chaplin films were shot.

In this morning's newspapers there is a report that Evo Morales, the uncynical and relatively open-hearted President of Bolivia, has proposed a new law which will make it legal for kids to start working as soon as they are 10 years old. Nearly a million Bolivian kids are at the moment doing such illicit work in order to contribute to their families having enough to eat. His law will grant them a little legal protection.

Six months ago, in the sea around the Italian island of Lampedusa, 400 immigrants from Africa and the Middle East were drowned in an unseaworthy boat whilst trying to enter Europe clandestinely in the hope of finding jobs. Across the planet 300 million men, women and children are looking for work in order to have the bare minimum to survive. The Tramp has become legion.

The extent of the apparently inexplicable increases day by day. The politics of universal suffrage have become meaningless because the discourse of national politicians no longer has any connection with what they do or can do. The fundamental decisions determining today's world are all being taken by financial speculators and their agencies, who are nameless and politically speechless. As the 10-year-old presumed: 'Words are missing to name or explain the daily run of trouble, unmet needs and frustrated desire.'

The clown knows that life is cruel. The ancient jester's motley coloured costume turned his usually melancholy expression into a joke. The clown is used to loss. Loss is his prologue.

The energy of Chaplin's antics is repetitive and incremental. Each time he falls, he gets back on to his feet as a new man. A new man who is both the same man and different. The secret of his buoyancy is his multiplicity.

The same multiplicity enables him to hold on to his next hope, although he is used to his hopes being repeatably shattered. He undergoes humiliation after humiliation with equanimity:

even when he counter-attacks, he does so with a hint of regret. Such equanimity renders him invulnerable – invulnerable to the point of seeming immortal. We, sensing this immortality in our hopeless circus of events, acknowledge it with our laughter.

In Chaplin's world Laughter is immortality's nick-name.

There are photos of Chaplin in his mid-80s. Looking at them one day, I found the expression on his face familiar. Yet I didn't know why. Later it came to me. I checked it out. His expression is like Rembrandt's in his last self-portrait: *Self-portrait as a Laughing Philosopher or as Democritus.*

'I'm only a little nickel comedian,' he says; 'all I ask is to make people laugh.'

ET IN ARCADIA EGO

Scandinavia is sparsely populated and when its inhabitants live closely side by side or come together to form a crowd, they resist becoming a mass. In the strict physical sense of the term they remain incoherent. This reluctance to merge, or this need to remain separate, is not a simple expression of individualism, for the same people are in other ways obedient, civic-minded and conventional. The Calvinist conscience may have something to do with it. But there is something else too, which is not in the least Calvinist. They all inherit a certain ideal of a wayward happiness, an ideal sustained by a shared memory, partly invented, partly true, of childhood summers, of sun and water and of days that never end. All cultures invent their own Arcadia, but this arcadia is closely connected with the region's climate and geography. Its winters are intolerably long and dark, and annually the two months of summer, with their more or less white nights – depending upon the exact longitude – are like a physically earned reward, like a declaration of innocence.

As I write these words, I suddenly think of the paintings Sven made ten years ago on the island of Belle-Isle, off the coast of Brittany. Naked bodies, surf, salt water sluicing off rocks, a sparkling sunlight touching everything, no end in sight. They are, in fact, images of that wayward happiness and those childhood summers.

In the Scandinavian summer people of all ages take off as many clothes as their self-respect permits, so that the three innocences of sunlight, water and rewarded bodies can touch.

I came to Stockholm to attend his funeral.

We were friends for fifty years and we did many things together. We mended roofs. We cooked. We collaborated on books. We travelled. We mixed cement. We went on demonstrations. Sometimes we read the same book in the same week so as to discuss it. What Sven was politically has not yet been named – maybe it will be in the next twenty years, when the world transformations taking place today are better understood. For want of a better term, he was content to be called an anarchist. Had he been labelled a terrorist, he would have shrugged his shoulders.

He had a swinging walk, as if his torso was riding a camel. He spoke rather slowly and his voice was exceptionally reassuring – the voice of a man whispering to you in confidence that a cease-fire has been announced. When he insisted upon a point, when he became intransigent and – when he still had it – his hair stood on end! His long bony fingers ended in particularly large finger tips which somehow promised that he could distinguish quality blindfold. And this also re-assured both women and men.

Although thin and tall, he swam with the ease and grace of a porpoise.

On the day before the funeral. I went to the National Museum in Stockholm, to look at paintings we had once looked at together. There was a Berthe Morisot landscape he particularly liked. It's painted like the inside of a dress, he said, the inside of a dress touching the skin!

The summer of about forty years ago was the first time I lived for several months in Sven and Romaine's house in the Vaucluse. Their daughter Karin had just been born. The house, with two fig trees, surrounded by cherry and apricot orchards, was primitive; there was no electricity and no tap water. There was collected rain water for washing in, and the drinking water we fetched from a fountain in the village. The cooking we did on a hearth in the kitchen. At midday when it was hot the chickens came into the kitchen for shade. There were also two dogs. Romaine worked outside, chiselling local stone and making sculptures. She was often covered in white dust. Sven painted in a kind of upstairs shed. The one luxury of the four roomed house was a library – a room lined with books belonging to Sven – where I worked. All the money we had was kept in a bowl on the mantelpiece above the hearth in the kitchen. Everywhere the sound of cicadas and at night the screech of owls. It was not at all Scandinavian, but Sven brought his arcadia with him, and in July and August we paid the price, since more and more visitors came and did not want to leave. They slept in the grass or put up tents.

Sven and I cooked and served the evening meal. We used only enamel plates because they were easier for stacking and did not break. People had to sit on the stones Romaine would one day sculpt or the removed seats from a Citroen 2cv. The guests came from Paris, Germany, London, Stockholm. They were scientists, professors, doctors, art historians, architects, and they all believed – such was Sven's presence, welcome and sleight of hand – that they had fallen (by accident) into Paradise.

Seven visitors have been here since mid-afternoon. We hear another carload coming along the dirt-track which leads to the house. The house had formerly belonged to an old peasant who, when he was dying, gave it to Sven to cheat the State. I look at my watch. We'll have Menu C tonight, Sven says to me confidentially. I'll light the fire, you go!

Menu C means that I drive to the public rubbish dump in Cavaillon and pick out the still edible vegetables and fruit, thrown away when the market closed. Before leaving the kitchen I take money from the bowl to buy bread.

In the National Museum was a Rembrandt which I'd never seen before and which wasn't there when we went round the museum together. The subject is Simeon, the old man, presenting the infant Jesus in the Temple. Soon he will say his famous Nunc Dimittis.

My wanting to try to do a drawing of the painting had nothing however to do with words. I simply wanted to look closer at the way the swaddled child was lying like a fish across the old man's outstretched forearms, with the thumbs and eight fingers of the two hands almost but not quite touching.

Sven was a full-time painter for over sixty years, and during that time he sold fewer paintings than any other artist I've ever known. As a result, he faced considerable material difficulties. He always lacked money. Most of his life he lacked what the most modest painter would think of as a proper studio. And, except by a few friends, he was unrecognized. Nevertheless scarcely a day passed when he did not pick up a brush, pastel, or pen to work, and on many days he worked until the hours counted no more, and he stepped into the innocence of that season where nature can be taken by surprise.

I always had the impression Sven didn't choose his subjects; it was they who placed orders. His subjects became his patrons: a coastline, a cherry orchard, a river crossing a city, a range of mountains, the gnarled branches of a vine, the face of a friend.

During the last few years when he was suffering from advanced Parkinson's disease, his patron, on every day he felt strong enough, would be a plate of fruit which he arranged with his long trembling fingers on the corner of a table in the flat where he lived with his family in the centre of Stockholm. Of these fruit he made still-lives, scarcely larger than postcards, using oil-sticks.

He considered it a waste of time to talk of his difficulties, because he believed in Providence. He counted on happy accidents (of course you have to recognize them when they happen, he points out), the example of Pissarro who had a heart of gold as well as being a great painter, unexpected encounters (a question of keeping your eyes open; most people don't) and natural mystery. This is why on his last, very small, still lives the colours speak to one another. It is also why he lived without resentment. He could become angry but he personally resented nothing. And when he listened to Bach, his belief in Providence was deeply confirmed.

Those who disapproved of Sven thought him pigheaded. He never retracted, never openly changed an opinion. He continually edged forward. Even during the final months when, unassisted, he could only move forward twenty centimetres by twenty centimetres, and five metres was an impossibly long distance, he continually edged forward, or else he rested, with his eyes shut, until he found the strength to do so. Others disapproved of him because he devoted his whole life to art, and they saw he was not a genius. For them, the nobility of that persistence passed unnoticed.

He died, alone, of a heart attack, a few metres

away from the table where he arranged the little plates of fruit for his still lives. It was the longest day of the year, 21 June 2003. When his body was discovered, the days were already getting minimally shorter.

The funeral was to take place at 2 p.m. in a southern suburb called Skogskyrkogården. We decided to take the metro and eat a sandwich there before going to the designated chapel. After half-an-hour's wait a train arrives and we climb in. All the men are in shorts and the women have bare shoulders. It is very hot. Through the coach, as it rocks on its way with all its windows open, wafts a tolerance for clumsy love, inelegance, missed opportunities, freckled backs, strange murmurs, sweaty hair, hot feet: life as it is.

Where we arrive there are two flower shops and a cemetery which appears to go on for ever. We each buy a rose to place on the coffin. There is nowhere to buy anything to eat. For that we have to take the metro back to the last station, which is at the beginning of the cemetery.

This is what we do. More flower shops, and

in front of them a complex of modern flats, built around a lawned square. By the entrance to this inner square I spot a sign announcing a restaurant, with an arrow. We follow it, hoping to find a sandwich. Many tables and a self-service counter. A menu of boiled hake with white sauce and boiled potatoes. A big display of sweet cakes and coloured pastries like toys, from which to choose a dessert. Coffee. Tea. Apple juice or what they call *small beer* (2% alcohol). Many of the people in the waiting queue have sticks. Everything in the canteen is white, glossy white – like a white metal drawer for cutlery. And there is a faint smell of rubber tubing. Three more clients arrive in wheelchairs. The man behind me, as I hesitate about what to drink, says: Small beer is better than nothing!

A few minutes later I notice a man and a woman in white uniforms wearing plastic gloves and carrying drip-feed bottles, and put two and two together. We are in the canteen for flats reserved for old people who, thanks to on-site medical care, still manage to live by themselves. Their canteen is also open to the public.

Each diner has chosen to sit at a different table. They preserve their independence like passengers in a station waiting room. Their common destination is behind the florists across the road.

They keep their eyes lowered, studying what is on their plates. To watch day by day the evident solitude of each of the others is probably harder to bear than one's own solitude. The one exception is the Small beer man who wanders from table to table, repeating: Another hot day! and then, grinning, decides to join us at our table just as we are on the point of leaving so as not to be late for the funeral.

Outside the air is as hot as a panting horse's breath, and the cemetery and its stillness extend as far as the eye can see.

After the funeral, the hundred or so people attending were invited to a buffet-meal in the garden, outside the building in which Sven had been allotted a municipal studio. At one moment I left the garden and opened the door I remembered on the ground floor. The studio was uncannily tidy. The tidiness bespoke his absence. There was nothing on the easel. A number of canvasses were visible instead of being face to the wall; the strong ones looked stronger, and the weaker ones looked desolate. What astounded me most, however, was the large reproduction pinned at eye level to the wall which was facing the easel. It was the Rembrandt Simeon.

I rejoined the family and guests drinking wine in the garden, and asked about the reproduction, but nobody was sure when Sven had acquired it and pinned it there. It is thought to be the last painting Rembrandt worked on.

The day after the funeral we drove north towards the archipelago on an old Yamaha 550 cc bike which a Swedish friend had lent me. The archipelago, with its abundance of islands, straits, sounds, peninsulas and bays, somehow copies the topography of Memory, and thus easily lends itself to being the dream site of legendary childhoods. These childhoods contain nautical skills and a familiarity with sailing that are not dreamlike, and it's through these practices – the tying of knots, the trimming of sails, the beaching of boats, the skills of using a tiller – that the arcadian dream feeds off a traditional reality. Come to the archipelago and every man over fifty-five puts on a cap which pretends he was once a sea captain.

On the bike we were heading north for the island of Furusund which is 3 kilometres long and about 1 kilometre wide.

At the southeast corner of the island there's a landing stage, a shop, a café, and many fair haired, bare legged giants – both women and men – who lick ice creams very slowly, read the sky, fill up their launches with petrol, carry their towels to take showers because they've been swimming far out at sea, and let their toddlers in lifejackets pace the decks of their boats unaccompanied.

It is late afternoon. Beside us a sea captain in shorts has offered an ice cream to a young boy whom I noticed playing with a football. He has very smart feet.

I saw a moose this morning, says the boy to the captain.

I doubt it at this time of year.

I did.

How many branches did it have?

I didn't have time to count – it ran off.

At this point the two of them stop and look towards the water. A ship has appeared sailing north along the channel between Furusund and Yxlan.

The scale of this ship is unfathomable. She is taller than four forests placed one on top of the other. She passes silently, as if her improbability has been able to pierce the visible but not the audible. She will arrive in Helsinki tomorrow morning, just after the sun has lit up a four-storey yellow building there, before which she will dock.

How did your moose get on the island? asks the sea captain.

It swam, replies the boy, must have swum.

Moose move around in herds. They are not loners, and they don't swim in the sea.

Then this one must have been lost. I saw him between the trees; he was an old one.

I join the people, the children and the dogs on the quayside. All of them are standing and looking up with astonishment at the improbably large and silent white ship, an astonishment which is habitual, for the same ship or sister ship passes every evening at the same hour.

I travelled on this line fifteen years ago. And I drove a bike off the ship by the four-storey yellow building in Helsinki. I was writing a novel then and I incorporated the ship into the story. I described her as the vessel which transports the dead across the Styx.

If we knew how our stories risk catching up with us, would we write differently? I think not. But at that moment on the ship I, as storyteller, was the decider of destinies. I was the navigator. I might even have been invited on to the captain's bridge. Whereas now on the island of Furusund I look up at the same ship passing and feel as small as everyone else. The few passengers on deck look down at us from something like the height of a suspension bridge. And only I know that Sven is on board.

I walk between some birches, listen to the special sound the leaves of trees make when they are growing beside salt water. Then I return to the café.

Is the weather going to stay the same? the boy asks the captain.

Yes, it'll be fine tomorrow.

Tomorrow I'm going to look for the moose before the sun's up.

The white ship has passed the northern point of Furusund and has vanished.

A week later in the Haute Savoie, I'm cooking fish on a wood fire outside and my son, Yves, brings me a glass of wine to drink and holds out a bowl of olives. It's getting dark and my eyes are sore from the smoke, so I feel for a couple with my fingers without looking, and pop one into my mouth. As I spit out the stone and try to define the flavour – sharp, bitter-black, Greek – a thought crosses my mind: From now on I taste olives for Sven too.

And suddenly, rubbing my eyes, I remember: Sven and I first met by chance and swapped addresses in a large Poussin exhibition in London where, amongst many others, the painting *Et in Arcadia ego* was hanging. The canvas shows a shepherdess and three arcadian shepherds, brought up short by a tomb, which is the last thing they were expecting to come upon there. One of them is reading out the inscription on the gravestone to the others.

Wonderful! Sven said, his hair standing on end. Everything in the painting leads the eye to the shadow of the arm of the one who's reading the words! You see? This shadow here! And he pointed.

ON VIGILANCE

Many people have their favourite bars where they like to meet friends and share a drink. I prefer drinking with friends at home. But I do have my favourite municipal swimming pools, where I go to swim up and down at my own pace, crossing other swimmers whom I don't know, although we exchange glances and sometimes smiles.

The wearing of bathing caps is obligatory. As is also a shower with shampoo before diving or stepping down a corner ladder into the pool. I dive, and as I swim my first strokes under water I have the sensation of having entered another timeframe, somewhat similar to the feeling a child may have at home when he decides to go from one floor to another.

As swimmers we share a kind of egalitarian anonymity. No shoes, no marks of rank. Just our swimming costumes. If you accidentally touch another swimmer whilst passing him or her, you offer an apology. The limitless cruelty towards others like ourselves, the cruelty of which we are capable when we are regimented and indoctrinated, is difficult to imagine here as you turn to swim your twentieth length.

The outside walls and the flat roof of the municipal pool are of glass. So from the water you can see the surrounding buildings and the sky. To the west there is a slope of grass at the top of which grows a large, tall silver-maple tree. I watch this tree as I swim on my side.

The overall form of the tree, with its many upward thrusting branches, is like the shape of any one of its leaves. (This is more or less evident for most varieties of tree.) The maple leaf is pinnate shaped – from *pinna*, the Latin for feather. The face of the leaf is a salad green, its back a greenish silver. The inscribed destiny of the maple is to be pinnate.

I decide to make a drawing of it as soon as I get out of the pool: a sketch of the whole tree and on the same page a close-up drawing of one of its leaves. Like this, I say to myself, still swimming, it will refer in some way to the maple's genetic code. It'll be a kind of text of a silver maple tree.

Such texts belong to a wordless language which we have been reading since early childhood, but which I cannot name.

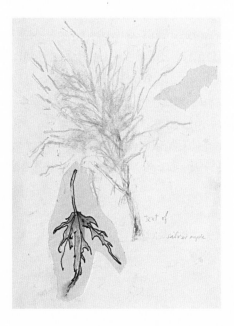

Later I swim on my back and look up at the sky through the framed glass roof. A vivid blue with white cirrus clouds at an altitude, I'd guess, of about 5000 metres. (The Latin for curl is *cirrus*.) The curls slowly shift, join, separate as the clouds drift in the wind. I can measure their drift thanks to the roof frame; otherwise it would be hard to notice it.

The movement of the curls apparently comes from inside the body of each cloud, not from an applied pressure; you think of the movements of a sleeping body.

This is probably why I stop swimming, and put my hands behind my head and float. My big toes just break through the surface. The water below holds me.

The longer I gaze at the curls the more they make me think of wordless stories; wordless stories like the stories fingers may tell, but in fact

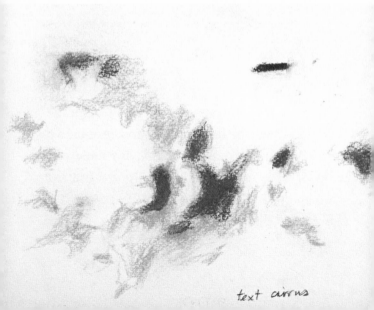

text cirrus

here stories told by minuscule ice crystals in the silence of the blue.

Yesterday I read in the newspaper that in Gaza twenty Palestinians were blown to pieces in their homes; that the USA has covertly dispatched 300 more troops to defend their interest in Iraq's oil refineries; that James Foley, an American journalist held hostage by Isis, was beheaded and a video of his execution uploaded to the internet; and that 35 illegal immigrants from India, men, women and children, were found suffocating in a shipping-container on a freighter that had just crossed the North Sea to dock in London.

The cirrus is drifting northwards towards the deep end of the pool. Afloat on my back, motionless, I watch it and chart with my eyes the pattern of its undulations.

Then the assurance the sight offers changes. It takes me time to understand how. Slowly the change becomes evident and the assurance I receive becomes deeper. The curls of the white cirrus are observing a man afloat on his back with his hands behind his head. I'm no longer observing them; they are observing me.

A MEETING PLACE

In my hands
From past and future
I'll grab two stones
And run with them.
Even in the lightest breeze I'll fly,
Summon a wind, to come
And wipe out every trace
And I'll sit like an orphan
By the roadside, mourning
My two stones.

Recently I began reading the Iraqi poet Abdulkareem Kasid and I go on reading and rereading him. I find his voice deeply impressive and highly relevant to what is happening in the world today.

I read him in English, translated from the Arabic by the poet himself, his daughter and a friend.

75

This cat –
Does it eavesdrop
On my chatter ?

He was born in Basra in 1946. Today he lives
in London.

His voice, the stories he conjures up, the way
he questions, makes me think of the experience
of being in a desert. There are spots in a desert
where the space between sand and sky seems to
be infinite, and there are other spots where
there seems to be no space, and land and sky
appear to be joined. If one walks through them,
however, the touch of the air on one's upright
body is the same in both cases. And the touch of
Kasid's words on one's imagination is like that.

Poem after poem describes being stranded,
but in each poem the reader is touched by the
presence of a past and a future.

Today most analyses and commentaries about
events – about terrorism, about migration and
economic insecurity, start their accounts too
recently. The entire world altered fundamentally
during the last decade of the twentieth century,
during the 1990s.

It was then that the agencies, the lobbies, the multinational organizations of speculative financial capitalism became the supreme decision-makers concerning the evolution of the globe. Hence globalization.

The dogma of neo-liberalism has rendered classical politics obsolete. Parliamentary politicians have become powerless; all they can do is talk. The media took over the same empty, vacuous language. Terms such as Europe, International solidarity, Independence, have become obsolete and unsubstantial. And the proliferation of acronyms in global reporting reflects this same drift towards insubstantiality.

What now keeps the world turning is the next immediate acquisition: the next Deal and Loan for finance; the next purchase for consumers.

Any sense of History, linking past and future, has been marginalized, if not eliminated. And so, people are suffering a sense of Historic loneliness. The French refer to those who are forced to live in the street as S. D. F. Sans Domicile Fixe. We are under a constant pressure to feel that we may have become the S. D. F. of History. There are no longer any acknowledged occasions for us to receive the dead and the unborn. There is each day's life, yet what surrounds it is a void. A void in which millions of us are today alone. And such solitude can transform Death into a companion.

Kasid, and the tradition to which he belongs as a poet, is not nostalgic about the past, any more than it is utopian about the future. Kasid frequents history – as if it were a meeting place – not to prove any argument – but for company.

> A café in the distance –
> I see it now as a tree
> Its roof made of branches and leaves
> Chairs made of wood.
> The people who go there like to sit down
> Lightly, on the branches.

LA LALALA LALALA LA

Along a seaside promenade, signs announce that dogs are strictly forbidden on the beach. It is early October. There are no swimmers. People, however, are strolling along the sand and a few are sunbathing. More than half of them are accompanied by dogs. We are in Italy.

The beach is on the outskirts of the fishing town of Comacchio in the delta of the river Po. Venice is sixty km to the north, Ravenna thirty km to the south.

There is water in whichever direction you look. Salt water from the sea, fresh water from the arms of the great river. Half-island, half-lagoon, it's a place which seems to belong to no continent. Everyone here – men, women and children – can handle a boat.

In the town there are as many canals as streets. The economy of the place depends upon fishing and, above all, on eels – on catching, preparing, smoking and exporting eels as a gastronomic delicacy.

All the town's trades are connected with water, and the isolation which this implies perhaps explains the physique of its inhabitants. The women and men of Comacchio are recognizably different from their neighbours. Stocky, broad-shouldered, weather-tanned, big-handed, used to bending down, used to pulling on ropes and bailing out, accustomed to waiting, patient. Instead of calling them down-to-earth, we could invent the term: down-to-water.

Every year in the first week of October they celebrate a fête known as the *Sagra dell'Anguilla* (the Festival of the Eel). The cobbled town centre is crammed with stalls of street-sellers, come from elsewhere, selling trinkets, rings, sea shells, cheeses, madonnas, salamis, dolls at low prices, small pleasures. The inhabitants wander slowly past, fingering the knickknacks, reckoning the small pleasures and from time to time paying out a few coins. There are also benches and trestle tables where one can drink and eat. There is the smell of food being grilled. Onions, aubergines, peppers and, of course, eels.

The eels when they are caught are a mercury silver, about 40 cm long and usually more than ten years old. When they are younger and smaller they are yellow. Before that, when they are newly hatched, they are transparent *leptocephali*, smaller than tadpoles. They hatch out deep in the Sargasso sea, opposite Mexico. It takes them three or four years to cross the Atlantic, following the Gulf Stream and to arrive at the mouth of the Po.

There they exchange salt water for fresh water, settle in the wetlands of Comacchio and grow large. After a number of years the urge comes over them in the autumn to return to the ocean bed they originally came from and to spawn. Having spawned, they die there amongst the Sargasso seaweed; the new, tiny transparent *leptocephali* then re-cross the ocean alone.

It is when the fully grown eels are leaving the wetlands of Comacchio each autumn that most of them are caught. As they set out to rejoin the salt sea, they unknowingly swim into the traps cunningly arranged by the fishermen. These traps they call the *lavoriero*.

This afternoon, apart from those working and selling at the fair, nobody is working. The boats are moored and still.

In the Piazza x x settembre, beside the medieval bell-tower, a folk group is setting up. There's a drummer, a violinist, a double bass, a flautist and a male singer. Three men and two women with their cables, mikes, instruments, lights, music-stands, clutter. All of them are wearing either trousers or skirts of the same tartan. Their legs and arms are bare. It's hot.

Michele the male singer mouths a syllable to the other players, takes the guitar and strikes a note. Lilia picks it up on her flute. The sound is so full of promise you catch on straightaway why Plato, the idealist, banished the instrument from his city-state. Michele's voice lets out the words syllable by syllable and between them his body swings.

Some passers-by stop to listen. Then others pause and stop. An eight-year-old girl and a boy of four begin to dance on the cobbles between players and public. They are the kids of one of the musicians.

The listeners form a half circle and, encouraged by Michele, start clapping to the beat and swaying to the rhythm.

What Laia is doing with her violin, as she turns in circles, head bent forward as if she were giving suck to a baby who is drawing out, not milk, but notes, a hundred people are now following with their humming and stomping.

They don't have musical instruments but what they are playing on and improvising with are their own sensations and convictions about being alive at the moment when this day is ending and the evening beginning.

How do the *leptocephali* find their way over the ocean-bed to the river's mouth? If they are remembering something, it is something that occurred before they existed.

What do they follow?

How does the music being played and improvised in the Piazza xx settembre find its way with equal assurance into the hearts of a hundred or more unique and diverse lives? What is it listening to beneath itself?

I have just learnt that Cesaria Evora has died. It was not until she was in her 50s that she became known to the world. She sang black West African Portuguese songs in a language and with an accent that was incomprehensible to most people who were not from Cape Verde. She was intransigent, obstinate, recidivist. The pitch of her voice was that of a teenager trying her luck in a bar for sailors, before going home to look after her sick mother. 'Every dog has his Friday' she once said.

When she tours the world – the present tense is obligatory – she fills the gigantic stadiums, yet she isn't exotic; she is poor. She has a round face like a bosom. When she smiles, which she often does, it is a smile that comes after the tragic has been assimilated. The rich listen to songs; the poor cling to them and make them their own. Life, Evora said, consists of gall and honey. She sings our incomprehensible lives to us.

In the Piazza xx settembre the song ends and gives way to a waiting silence. The musicians consult and get their breath back. The throng from Comacchio stand there relaxed, leaning against the silence as if it was a wall. Newcomers join them. Some shake hands or touch a shoulder.

Then they all wait as they do for the tidal water to rise before climbing into and pushing off in one of their flat-bottomed boats.

While they are waiting, I want to go thirty kilometres south to the Basilica of Sant'Apollinare in Classe, outside Ravenna, and there I want to show you a basin mosaic in the sixth century apse. It has the form of a scallop shell, a good ten metres in diameter, enclosing about the same space as the folk group occupy in the Piazza xx settembre.

The basin mosaic shows the earth and sky, with trees, birds, grass, stones, sheep. At the top is the open hand of God, no larger than a pebble. In the centre is the head of Christ, no larger than the palm of God's small hand. The principal colours are greens, white, gold and a turquoise blue. Its nominal subject is the Transfiguration of Christ on Mount Tabor in Galilee. And the mosaic transfigures space. Each entity we see – be it a flower, a sheep, a tuft of grass, a pebble – is at the centre of the whole; nothing in the scene is marginal.

87

The arching mosaic evokes in terms of space something like what eternity may evoke in terms of time. It simultaneously contains and abolishes space. Distance here brings together instead of separating.

How does it achieve such a transfiguration? The secret is in the way the mosaic's tesserae play with the light. These tiny cubic pieces of glass, marble and mineral generate, because of how they are placed together, an extraordinary visual energy. How do they do this?

The tesserae vary in their different tints of the same colours. No two are quite the same. The angle at which they were inserted into the mortar fourteen centuries ago also varies, sector by sector, and this means that the light they reflect is in places bright and in other places opaque – as happens in nature when light is reflected off moving water. And, finally, the lines of the tesserae – the convoys in which they pro-ceed across the curved mosaic – are never straight but always more or less serpentine. They proceed like eels.

When you look up and watch the whole mosaic, everything you see is motionless and calm, and at the same time part of a ceaseless orbital spin.

This is why each entity – each tree or flower or sheep or stone or prophet – wherever it has been placed and whatever its size – becomes, when you watch it, the centre of everything surrounding it.

The song they choose next in the Piazza XX settembre is 'Il Pescatore'. It was written and first sung in the 1970s by Fabrizio De André. For two generations kids all over Italy hummed and sang it.

The song tells the story of an old fisherman asleep on a beach. His face is creased, furrowed in a smile. Another guy appears. He is on the run. He begs for bread to ease his hunger and wine to quench his thirst. Without hesitation the fisherman gives him both. The man goes on his way. Two mounted police arrive on the beach and ask the fisherman whether he has seen anybody. The fisherman, as the sun goes down, says nothing.

The story is forlorn; the tune, the voice, the rhythm are gregarious and reassuring. Between each two verses there's a refrain: la lalala lalala la . . .

Michele extends his arms and a hundred listeners sing the refrain together. The medieval wall, visible behind them – between their shoulders and heads – turns to gold until the refrain ends. Then it returns to being stone.

SOME NOTES ABOUT SONG
(for Yasmine Hamdan)

When I was watching and listening to you performing last week, Yasmine, I had an impulse to draw you. An absurd impulse because it was too dark; I couldn't see the sketchbook on my knees. At moments I scribbled without looking down or taking my eyes off you.

There's a rhythm in these scribbles – as though my pen was accompanying your voice. But a pen isn't a mouth-organ or a fiddle, and now in the silence my scribbles mean almost nothing.

You were wearing red shoes with heels, black tight leggings, a dark, brownish, half-transparent tee shirt with padded shoulders and an orange shawl, the colour of apricots. You looked as though you weighed very little, dry, sparse, like a perpetual wanderer.

When you began to sing, this changed. Your

entire body, no longer dry, was filled with sound, as a bottle can be filled to overflowing with liquid.

You sang in Arabic, a language I don't understand, and yet I received each song, not as a partial, but as a complete experience. How to explain this? To suggest that the words of a song don't matter is plain stupid; they are the seeds from which it has grown.

I received each song you sang as did a hundred or more other people, very few of whom

94

were Arabic-speaking. We were able to share with you what you were singing. How to explain this? I'm not sure I can, but I want to make some notes.

A song, when being sung and played, acquires a body. And it does this by taking over and briefly possessing existent bodies. The body of the double bass standing vertical whilst it's being strummed, or the body of the mouth-organ cupped in a pair of hands hovering and pecking like a bird before a mouth, or the torso of the drummer as he rolls. Again and again it takes over the body of the singer. And after a while the body of the circle of listeners who, as they listen and gesture to the song, are remembering and foreseeing.

A song, as distinct from the bodies it takes over, is unfixed in time and place. A song narrates a past experience. When it is being sung it fills the present. Stories do the same. But songs have another dimension which is uniquely theirs. A song while filling the present hopes to reach a listening ear in some future somewhere. It leans forward, further and further. Without the persistence of this hope, songs, I believe, would not exist. Songs lean forward.

The tempo, the beat, the loops, the repetitions of a song construct a shelter from the flow of linear time: a shelter in which future, present and past can console, provoke, ironize and inspire one another.

Most songs being listened to across the world at this moment are recordings – not live performances. And this means that the physical experience of sharing and coming together is less intense, but it is still there in the heart of the exchange and communication taking place.

> Good mornin', blues,
> blues, how do you do?
> How do you do?
> Good mornin', blues,
> blues, how do you do?
> Say, I just come here
> to have a few words with you.
>   (Bessie Smith)

The song I most remember my mother singing is Shenandoah. She would sometimes sing at the end of a meal when there were guests and if there was a moment of silent plenitude. She had a soft alto voice, melodious, never dramatic. The song, which was in my father's songbook, dates from the mid-nineteenth century. The Shenandoah valley was a site of Indian settlements in the middle of the United States.

Oh Shenandoah
I long to see you,
away you rolling river,
Oh Shenandoah
I long to see you,
Away, I'm bound away
'cross the wide Missouri.

Shenandoah was the name of a Native American chief, and a river, a tributary to the Missouri which joins the Mississippi. It became a song often sung by blacks because the Missouri separated the slave-owning South of America from the North. It was also a song boatmen and sailors liked to sing. The lower reaches of the Missouri were in those days a river with much navigation.

My mother sang it to me when I was one or two years old. Not often, it was not a ritual, and I have no precise memory of her singing to me alone. But the song was there. A mysterious object among others in the house and I was aware of it being there – like a shirt in a wardrobe, for special occasions.

'Tis seven years
since last I've seen you
and hear your rolling river.

'Tis seven years
since last I've seen you.
Away, we're bound away.
Across the wide Missouri

In every song there is distance. The song is not distant, but distance is one of its ingredients, just as presence is an ingredient of any graphic image. This has been true from the beginning of songs and the beginning of images.

All songs are about journeys.

I wish I was in Carrickfergus
only for nights in Ballygran
I would swim over the deepest ocean –
The deepest ocean – to be by your side.

Songs refer to aftermaths and returns, welcomes and farewells. Or to put it another way: songs are sung to an absence. Absence is what inspired them and it's what they address. At the same time (and the phrase 'at the same time' takes on a special meaning here) in the sharing of the song the absence is also shared and so becomes less acute, less solitary, less silent. And this 'reduction' of the original absence during the sharing of the singing, or even during the memory of such singing, is collectively experienced as something triumphant. Sometimes a mild triumph, often a covert one.

'I could wrap myself,' said Johnny Cash, 'in the warm cocoon of a song and go anywhere; I was invincible.'

Flamenco performers often talk about *el duende*. Duende is a quality, a resonance which makes a performance unforgettable. It occurs when a performer is possessed, inhabited, by a force or a set of compulsions coming from outside her or his own self. Duende is a ghost from the past. And it's unforgettable because it visits the present in order to address the future.

99

In the year 1933 the Spanish poet Garcia Lorca delivered a public lecture in Buenos Aires concerning the nature of el duende. Three years later, at the beginning of the Spanish Civil War, he was arrested in his home city of Granada and murdered, probably by General Franco's Guardia Civil.

'All the arts,' he pronounced in his lecture, 'are capable of duende, but where it naturally creates most space, as in music, dance and spoken poetry, the living flesh is needed to interpret them, since they have forms that are born and die perpetually, and raise their contours above the precise present. El duende works on the dancer's body like wind on sand. It changes a girl by magic power, into a lunar paralytic, or covers the cheeks of a broken old man, begging for alms in the wine shop, with adolescent blushes: gives a woman's hair the odor of a midnight sea port: and at every instant works the arms of a performer with gestures that are the mothers of all the dances of all the ages.'

There is always too much on my writing table, too many papers. The other day at the bottom of a pile I came across a postcard which a friend had sent me from Spain a couple of months before. The picture on it was a black and white photo of a Flamenco dancer, taken by the Spanish photographer Tato Olivas, famous for his pictures of dancers.

When I came across this image I felt something being triggered in my memory which I hadn't noticed when I first saw the postcard. I waited. Then it became clear.

The photo of the young woman about to

dance reminded me of a drawing I made of an iris. One of a series of drawings I made a couple of years before. I found the drawing and then compared the two.

Indeed there's something in common, an equivalence, between the geometry of the dancer's attendant body and the geometry of the opening flower. They have of course different features, but their energies and the way they are expressed in shapes, gestures and movements on the surface of the two images, are similar.

I scanned both images and put them together to make a diptych which I then sent with a letter to Tato Olivas.

He replied telling me he had taken the photo twenty years before in the famous Madrid school for Flamenco called Amor de Dios. It's now shut. He had never come across the dancer again and didn't know her name.

He went on to say that the 'coincidence' of the two images had made him think of another photo of his which was even closer to the iris drawing. A photo of the legendary dancer Sara Baros when she was young. He sent me a print of it. I couldn't believe my eyes.

The dancer and the iris are like twins except that one is a woman and the other a plant. You immediately assume that either the photographer or the draughtsman painstakingly set out to 'match' the other image. But this is not the case. The two images have never been placed side by side until now.

The likeness between them is inborn – as if it were genetic (which, in the normal sense of the term, it can't be). The energy of the Flamenco dance and the energy of the opening flower appear, however, to obey the same dynamic formula, to have the same pulse despite their very different time scales. Rhythmically they accompany one another; in evolutionary terms they are aeons apart.

'With gestures that are the mothers of all the dances of all ages.'

An Annunciation, painted by Antonello da Messina in the 1470s. It's a small oil painting, no larger than a modest mirror above a wash basin. In it there are no angels, no Gabriel, no olive branches, no lilies, no doves. We see the Virgin, close-up, head and shoulders, dressed in a blue robe and mantle. On a ledge in front of her is an open Psalter or prayer-book. She has just heard the announcement that she is to give birth to the son of God. Her eyes are wide open but she is looking inwards. Her lips too are open – she could be singing. Her two hands are pressing lightly but searchingly against her bosom. It is as though they want to touch, to finger her inside, her innards, which have heard a signal.

We have noted how a song borrows existent

physical bodies in order to acquire, while it's being sung, a body of its own. The borrowed body may be that of an instrument, of a single player, a group of players, a bunch of listeners. And the song shifts unpredictably from one borrowed body to another. What Antonello's painting can remind us of is that in each case the song settles in the *inside* of the body it borrows. It finds its place in the body's guts. In the drum of a drum, in the belly of a violin, in the torso or loins of singer and listener.

The essence of songs is neither vocal nor cerebral but organic. We follow them in order to be enclosed. And this is why what they offer is different from what is offered by any other message or form of exchange. We find ourselves inside a message. The unsung impersonal world remains outside on the other side of a placenta. All songs, even when their content or rendering are very strongly masculine, operate maternally.

Overleaf is a drawing by me of the hands in the painting by Antonello da Messina.

Songs connect, collect and bring together. Even when not being sung they are attendant assembly-points.

The words of songs are different from words which make prose. In prose, words are independent agents; in songs they are first and foremost the intimate sounds of their mother tongue. They signify what they signify, but at the same time they address or flow towards all the words which exist in that tongue.

Songs are like rivers. Each follows its own course – yet all are flowing to reach the sea from which everything came. The waters that flow out of a river's mouth are on their way to an immense elsewhere. And something similar happens with what comes out of the mouth of a song.

Much of what happens to us in life is name-less because our vocabulary is too poor. Most stories get told out loud because the storyteller hopes that the telling of the story can transform a nameless event into a familiar or intimate one.

We tend to associate intimacy with close-ness and closeness with a certain sum of shared experiences. Yet every day total strangers, who will never say a single word to one another, can share an intimacy. An intimacy contained in the exchange of a glance, a nod of the head, a smile, a shrug of a shoulder. A closeness which lasts for a second or for the duration of a song being sung and listened to together. An agreement about life. An agreement without clauses. A conclusion spontaneously shared between the untold stories gathered around the song.

Eight o'clock on a summer evening, in a metro train heading for a Parisian suburb. There are no empty seats but the standing passengers are not crammed together. Four men in their mid-twenties are standing in a group near the sliding doors on the right-hand side of the coach, the doors which don't open at stations when the train is running in this direction.

One of the group is black, two are white and the fourth is perhaps Maghrebian. I'm standing quite a distance away from them. What first caught my attention was their very visible connivance and the intensity of their conversation and storytelling.

The four – virile, masculine – are casually but scrupulously dressed. What they look like, their appearances, would seem to matter to them even more than to most men of their age. Everything about them is alert, nothing is hangdog. The Maghrebian is wearing loose blue shorts and spotless Nikes. The black man has cornrows the colour of sandalwood. All four are virile and masculine.

The train stops and a few passengers get out. I can move a little closer to the quartet.

Each intervenes frequently in the recital of each of the others. There are no monologues but equally nothing seems to be an interruption. Their fingers, very mobile, are often near their faces.

Suddenly it dawns on me that they are stone deaf. It was their fluency which prevented me from realizing this before.

Another station. They find four seats together. They continue to behave as if they were alone. Yet the manner in which they decide to ignore the rest of us is a form of tact and politeness, not of indifference.

Occasionally one of the four grunts with laughter. Their storytelling, their commentary on events continues. I am now watching them as curiously as they are watching each other.

Their shared vocabulary of gestural signs has its own syntax and grammar, mostly established by timing. These signs are made with their hands, faces and bodies which have taken over the function of both tongue and ear, of one organ which articulates and the other which receives. In any sustained dialogue anywhere both are equally important. Yet in the entire coach, probably in the entire train, there is no dialogue taking place, comparable to theirs.

Each physical feature with which the quartet gestures in order to converse – eye, upper lip, lower lip, teeth, chin, brow, thumb, finger, wrist, shoulder – each feature has for them the range of a musical instrument or of a voice, with all its specific notes, chords, trills and degrees of insistence and hesitancy.

Yet in my ears there is only the sound of the train which is slowing down for the next stop. Several passengers are getting to their feet. I could sit but I prefer to stay where I am. The quartet are of course aware of my presence. One of them gives me a smile, not of welcome, but of acquiescence.

Intercepting their myriad exchanges, to which I can give no name, following their responses back and forth while remaining ignorant about what they refer to, swinging to their rhythm, carried forward by their expectancy, I have the sensation of being surrounded by a song, a song born of their solitudes, a song in a foreign language. A song without sound.

This train is bound for glory, this train,
This train is bound for glory, and if you ride
it, it must be holy
   (Biddleville Quintette. Chicago, 1927)

Recently I listened to and watched the French President talking to the nation for almost three hours during a televised press conference. And his discourse was algebraic. That's to say logical and consequential, but with scarcely any reference to a tangible reality or to lived experience.

He has a sense of humour, he is intelligent, he gives the impression of being sincere, and of believing in the alliance with Big Business which he is proposing, although he was elected as a

Socialist candidate. Why is his discourse so vacuous? Why does it register like a monologue of acronyms?

It is because he has forsaken any sense of history, and therefore has no long-term political vision. Historically speaking, he lives from hand to mouth. He has abandoned hope. Hence the algebra. Hope engenders political vocabularies. Hopelessness leads to wordlessness.

In this Hollande is typical of the period we are living through. Most official discourses and commentaries are dumb concerning what is being lived and imagined by the vast majority of people in their struggles to survive.

The media offer trivial immediate distraction to fill the silence which, left empty, might otherwise prompt people to ask each other questions concerning the unjust world they are living in.

Our leaders and media commentators speak of what we are living through in a gobbledygook, which is not the voice of a turkey but that of High Finance.

It's difficult today to express or sum up in *prose* the experience of Being alive and Becoming.

Prose, as a form of discourse, depends upon a minimum of established continuities of meaning; prose is an exchange with a surrounding circle of different points of view and opinions, expressed in a shared and descriptive language. And such a shared language exists no more in most public discourse. A temporary but historical loss.

By contrast, songs can express the inner experience of Being and Becoming at this historic moment – even when they are old songs. Why? Because songs are self-contained and because songs put their arms around historic time.

> Takes a worried man to sing a worried song
> Takes a worried man to sing a worried song
> Takes a worried man to sing a worried song
> I'm worried nowwww
> But I won't be worried long.
>   (As sung by Woody Guthrie)

Songs put their arms around historic time without being utopian.

The enforced collectivization of the land

with the famine it caused in the Soviet Union and, later, the Soviet Gulag with its accompanying encyclopedias of double talk were initiated, relentlessly pursued and justified in the name of the utopia in which the new and unprecedented Soviet Man would soon live.

Likewise, today, the ever expanding human poverty and the ongoing pillaging of the planet are justified in the name of a utopia to be guaranteed by Market Forces, when they are unregulated and allowed to operate freely; a utopia in which, in Milton Friedman's words, 'each man can vote for the color of the tie he wants.'

In any utopian vision happiness is obligatory. This means that in reality it's unobtainable. Within their utopian logic compassion is a weakness. Utopias despise the present. Utopias substitute Dogma for Hope. Dogmas are engraved; hopes flicker, by contrast, like the flame of a candle.

Both candles and song often accompany prayer. And prayer in most, if not all, religions, temples and churches, is double-faced. It can endlessly reiterate dogma or it can articulate hope. And whichever it does, doesn't necessarily depend upon the place or circumstances where the prayer is being prayed. It depends upon the stories of those praying.

The small town of San Andrés Sakam'chen de los Pobres, in the state of Chiapas, in south Mexico. There's a small church there. From the church comes the faint sound of voices singing. Inside there's no priest. The four singers are standing. Two men and two young women. The four are indigenous Indians.

The men stand far apart from the women and all four are singing in polyphony. The two women have small babies attached to their backs.

In a side chapel there is a life-size statue of Saint Andrés, the apostle, carved in wood. He is dressed in a tunic and breeches which are not carved but are real clothes. On the floor of the church behind the altar are almost a thousand lit candles, many of them in small glass jars. A side-door has been left ajar; there is a draught of air which makes the candle flames quiver and lean sideways. The rhythm of the voices and the rhythm of the flickering candle flames.

Eventually one of the babies cries out to

be fed. The singing stops and the mother gives her baby her breast. The other woman, baby still sleeping, picks up the carrier bag at her feet, takes out a tunic, unfolds it and walks over to the statue of Saint Andrés. There she exchanges the tunic she has brought for the one the statue is wearing. As she foresaw, it needs to be washed.

The thousand candle flames still quiver in the draught.

I think now of Moya Cannon's remarkable poem:

It was always those with little else to carry
who carried the songs
to Babylon,
to the Mississippi –
some of these last possessed less than
    nothing
did not own their own bodies
yet, three centuries later, deep rhythms from
    Africa,
stowed in their hearts, their bones,
carry the world's songs.

For those who left my county,
girls from Downings and the Rosses
who followed herring boats north to Shetland
gutting the sea's silver as they went
or boys from Ranafast who took the Derry boat,
who slept over a rope in a bothy,
songs were their souls' currency
the pure metal of their hearts,

to be exchanged for other gold,
other songs which rang out true and bright
when flung down
upon the deal boards of their days.
   (Moya Cannon, *Carrying the Songs*,
   Carcanet Press)

The way singers play with or defy the linearity of time has something in common with what acrobats and jugglers do with the force of gravity. Recently in a French town I saw a family of tumblers performing on a street corner near a supermarket. A father, three boys and a girl. There was also a dog, a Scots terrier. The dog, I later found out, was called Nella and the father Massimo. All the kids were slim

117

and had dark eyes. Massimo was thick set and imposing.

The eldest boy who was probably seventeen, perhaps more (difficult to estimate their ages because for them there is no category of childhood) was the principal juggler and handler.

The young girl of six or seven climbed him as if he were a tree, a tree that then transformed itself into beams for a roof which she sat on. The father was standing a good way behind them, watching with eagle eyes as he strummed a guitar, an amplifier and sound gear on the paving stones between his feet. The roof beams became a lift which gently deposited Ariana the girl on the ground. The boy descended like a lift, very very slowly and the girl stepped back on the paving stones to the rhythm of her father's guitar.

Comes the moment for David (ten? eleven? years old) to do his number. There are only half a dozen spectators, it's midmorning, people are busy. David mounts his unicycle, rides it down the street, turns and rides back with the minimum of exertion. He does this to show his credentials.

Then, dismounting on to the sidewalk, he kicks off his trainers and steps on to a stuffed leather ball the size of a gigantic pumpkin. Pushing with his heels, and with the soles of his feet taking on the curvature of the ball, he slowly persuades it forward and the two of them advance. He keeps his arm down by his side. Nothing he does reveals the effort of maintaining his balance on the rolling ball.

He stands on it, chin up, looking into the far distance, like a statue on a plinth. The ball and he advance in triumph at the pace of a very slow tortoise. And at this moment of triumph, he begins to sing, accompanied by his father on a mouth-organ. David has a miniature mike attached with Scotch tape near his left cheekbone.

The song is Sardinian. He sings in an unruffled tenor voice. The voice of a solitary shepherd, not of a boy. The words describe what happens when a jinx is put on you, a story as old as the hills.

Triumph and jinx.

Jinx and triumph brought together in an act which, as you watch it, you hope will go on and on and on. Picasso painted the same act around the year 1900.

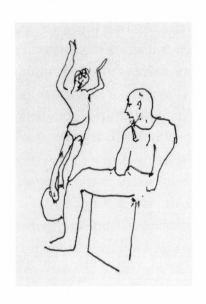

The jinx and the triumph. I have tried to explain why songs today can refer, in their own incomparable way, to everyone's experience of the world we are living in. And this, Yasmine, is how we can share with you what you are singing.

With your right hand you're holding the mike as though it might be swept away by a current. As your voice reaches a certain pitch you make a gesture with your left arm. You point it vertically at the floor where the cables coil beside your red shoes. And the thumb of your left hand is pointing vertically down to touch the tip, not of your first finger but of your second finger. Your first finger is bent double and pointing upwards to touch the pad of your thumb. We can't see its tip. And this gesture as your voice descends, singing your song about Samar's nights, announces that the muzzle of the song is nestling in the palm of your hand.

We begin to clap to your rhythm generating the energy and sharpening the shared attention necessary for heading elsewhere.

And suddenly, as we dared to hope, the elsewhere comes here to us through you.

PIECES OF SILVER

A few days ago I was standing in front of a painted image, measuring two metres by two, of paradise. And after a moment, standing still, gasping a little, I entered it.

Let me tell the story of what preceded this. I went to visit the studio of a painter friend of mine. We've known each other for about thirty years. In origin he's Czech. His name is Rostia. He lives in a Paris suburb of apartment blocks. His living accommodations and studio are in one such block, belonging to the local council. The rent he pays is low. The studio measures thirty square metres and is about six metres tall with a skylight. He and his wife sleep on a kind of balcony overlooking the studio floor.

I wanted to look at his recent paintings. Entering the studio was like entering a bunker

for soiled linen. Against all four walls were stacked canvases and gigantic stained sheets of thick paper, all the images painted on them facing the wall. The floor was covered with other paintings laid face down. No question of strolling around. I sat on a chair by the door.

Rostia, bare-foot, walked on the patched, crumpled sheets of paper on the floor and searched for something to show me. He unearthed a painting on paper, taller than him and wider than his outstretched arms, and he stapled it with a stapling gadget he asked me to pass him from under my chair – he stapled it to the back of a sketched canvas leaning against the far wall. It belonged to the series he had been working on for the last ten years. I look at it.

To visualize the perspectives contained in this series, imagine a helicopter flying low over a suburb or a favela or a zone of apartments blocks of four to six storeys, which cover an area of several kilometres, the lines of the streets sometimes straight and regular, and sometimes erratic with vacant lots and unfinished building sites. Rostia paints the aerial view.

I could show you a reproduction of one of these paintings but in our day and age reproductions no longer work; they deposit what they're showing in a colourful brochure of buyers' choices.

Intermingling with the rectangular apartment blocks with their repetitive square windows, are letters of the alphabet. They don't spell words; they are acronyms for unknown forces. Some are on ground level, others are in the sky.

Make no mistake, these paintings are not sinister; they are full of a thousand lives and a thousand solitudes. We recognize ourselves in them.

Rostia walks over the paintings on the floor to find another one to show me. He staples it to the back of a sketched canvas leaning against the wall beneath the balcony.

On this one is painted a shut book as large as the area covered by a dozen blocks, and the book floats, as silvery and light as a cloud, above the favela. I think of Tom Waits singing:

Everybody's talking at the same time
Well it's hard times for some
For others it's sweet
Someone makes money when there's blood
   in the street
Everybody's talking at the same time.

The pages of the book are pages of the lives below.

Rostia now finds a sketched canvas which shows the close-up head and shoulder of an adolescent who is in the helicopter, and the aerial view is around and behind him like a net or an internet screen.

Facebooks without end, but no horizon.

I must tell you about the colours. They are sombre; blacks, greys, sepias dominate, yet often they flash with silver in response to bright glimpses from other colours. The glimpses are like what you catch sight of at street level: a bit of blue sky, the potted flowers, carefully placed on the minuscule balconies which the apartment windows give on to, a bright set of puff garments on display in a store-window.

The colours in the paintings murmur and whisper and cat-call.

On one canvas the keyboard of an accordion plays with the streets and alleys beneath it. In another silvery reflections from a carafe and some drinking glasses wink at the apartment windows below. Never say Die!

He uses oil paint, collage, inks, aerosol. He has the kit of a graffiti artist and the eye of a master.

Rostia unravels a dozen more paintings. In the more recent ones there are again close-up faces, puzzling over the inconsequentiality of where they hang out down below.

That one is not finished, Rostia insists, though I've been working on it for years.

129

Now he wants to show me a finished smaller painting with more intense colours. Twenty such paintings are hanging one on top of the other, like towels on a rack in a corner of the studio. I know for sure that Rostia is one of the great painters of our time, but I've never succeeded in getting a curator or dealer to consider his work. His name? you ask. Kunovsky.

I want to show you the most recent and the largest, Rostia tells me, let's take it out of the studio. I think it's finished, he adds.

He fetches it from some hiding place – it's a sketched canvas of four square metres – and we proceed down a short corridor which gives on to a couple of shut doors. He leans it against the doors.

The perspective is exactly the same as in all the other paintings. The inconsequential suburb is below and there are some books on the shelves of the sky. One of the books is open. There are no cryptic acronyms; instead, high in the sky, there are the leaves, branches and fruit of a tree.

The helicopter has become an angel. Silver bubbles of breath sparkling with hope drift in the air. Colours comfort what were the greys. Each square window of the blocks below has become a soul.

I stood there speechless for a long while, then I entered it.

Such is art.

HOW TO RESIST A STATE
OF FORGETFULNESS

Last week Picasso's painting *Les Femmes d'Alger*, painted in 1955 (sixty years ago) was sold at Christie's in New York for 180 million dollars. Picasso's decision to paint it was, in part,

inspired by his wish to announce his support to the Algerian people in their struggle and their war, which had started the year before, against French colonialism.

Today is Ascension Day, forty days after Easter. According to the Gospels, it was the day when Christ, as witnessed by his disciples, ascended into the sky, into heaven. On the earth they were now on their own.

During the last week I've been drawing, mostly flowers, motivated by a curiosity which has little to do with either botany or aesthetics. I have been asking myself whether natural forms – a tree, a cloud, a river, a stone, a flower – can be looked at and perceived as messages. Messages – it goes without saying – which can never be verbalized, and are not particularly addressed to us. Is it possible to 'read' natural appearances as texts?

For me there is nothing mystical in this exercise. It is a gestural exercise, whose aim is to respond to different rhythms and forms of energy, which I like to imagine as *texts* from a language that has not been given to us to read. Yet as I trace the text I physically identify with

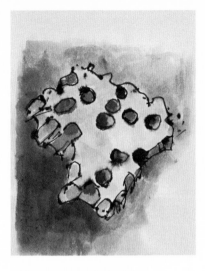

the thing I'm drawing and with the limitless, unknown mother tongue in which it is written.

In the totalitarian global-order of financial speculative capitalism under which we are living, the media ceaselessly bombard us with information, yet this information is mostly a planned diversion, distracting our attention from what is true, essential and urgent.

Much of the information is about what was once called politics, but politics have been superseded by the global dictatorship of speculative capitalism with its traders and banking lobbies.

Politicians, of both Left and Right, continue to debate, to vote, to pass resolutions, as if this were not the case. And, as a result, their discourse refers to nothing and is inconsequential. The words and terms they repeatedly use – such as terrorism, democracy, flexibility – have been emptied of any meaning. Their publics across the world follow their speaking heads as if they were glancing at an interminable school exercise or school class for learning Rhetoric! Bullshit.

Another chapter of the information with which we are bombarded concentrates on the spectacular: on shocking, violent events wherever they occur across the world. Robberies, earthquakes, capsized boats, insurrections, massacres. Once shown, one spectacle is replaced by another, deprived of context, in numbing succession. They come as shocks not stories. They are reminders of the unpredictability of what can happen. They demonstrate the risk factors in life.

Add to this the language used by the media to present and classify the world. It is very close to the jargon and logic of management experts. It *quantifies* everything and seldom refers to substance or quality. It deals with percentages, shifts in opinion-polls, unemployment figures, growth rates, mounting debts, estimates of carbon dioxide, et cetera, et cetera. It is a voice at home with digits but not with living or suffering bodies. It does not speak of regrets or hopes.

And so what is being publicly said and the way it is being said promotes a kind of civic and historic amnesia. Experience is being wiped out. The horizons of past and future are being blurred. We are being conditioned to live an

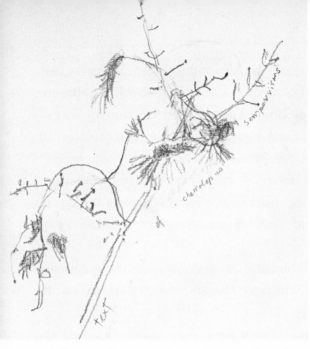

endless and uncertain present, reduced to being citizens in a state of forgetfulness.

Meanwhile, around us, the planet is overheating. The wealth of the planet is being concentrated in fewer and fewer hands; the majority are underfed, junk-fed or starving. More and more millions of people are being forced to emigrate with the slimmest hopes of survival. Working conditions are becoming more and more inhuman.

Those who are ready to protest against, and resist, what is happening today are legion, but the political means for doing so are for the moment unclear or absent. They need time to develop. So we have to wait. But how to wait in such circumstances? How to wait in this state of forgetfulness?

Let us recall that time, as Einstein and other physicists have explained, is not linear but circular. Our lives are not points on a line – a line which is today being amputated by the Instant Greed of the unprecedented global capitalist order. We are not points on a line; rather, we are the centres of circles.

The circles surround us with testaments addressed to us by our predecessors since the Stone Age, and by texts which are not addressed to us but which can be witnessed by us. Texts from nature, from the universe, and they remind us that symmetry co-exists with chaos, that ingenuities outflank fatalities, that what is desired is more reassuring than what is promised.

Then, sustained by what we have inherited from the past and what we witness, we will have the courage to resist and continue resisting in as

clematis text

yet unimaginable circumstances. We will learn how to wait in solidarity.

Just as we will continue indefinitely to praise, to swear and to curse in every language we know.

PICTURE CREDITS

p.37 *Boy Escaping* by Michael Quanne. (Photo © Christie's Images / Bridgeman Images)

p.38 *Broomfield House* by Michael Quanne. (© Michael Quanne)

p.43 *Self Portrait*, c.1668–9, by Rembrandt van Rijn. (Wallraf-Richartz Museum, Cologne, Germany/Bridgeman Images)

p.43 Charlie Chaplin (Sir Charles Spencer Chaplin, 1889–1977), English film actor and director, with his wife Oona O'Neill after receiving a Knighthood from Queen Elizabeth II at Buckingham Palace in London. (Photo by Fox Photos/Getty Images)

p.101 'Academia' (detail) by Tato Olivas.

p.103 'Sara Baras' (detail) by Tato Olivas.

145

p.107 *The Annunciation,* c.1473–74 by Antonello da Messina. Oil on panel. (Alte Pinakothek, Munich, Germany / Bridgeman Images)

p.126 Paradis by Rostislav Kunovsky. *From Nowhere* (2015). Techniques mixte sur toile, 200.

All other images are courtesy of the author.